My Philosophy Adventures with My Philosopher Grandfather

On Thinking

1

BUKET KURT

Illustrated by: Ece ZEBER
Translated by: Can Selin GULEL

With the support of
teda
the "Directions of the Ministry of Culture and Tourism Subvention Project for Dissemination of Turkish Cultural, Artistic and Literary Works into Foreign Languages (TEDA)"
Translation and Publication Grant Programme of Türkiye

My Philosophy Adventures with My Philosopher Grandfather : On Thinking

ISBN: 978-81-19745-59-3
Author: Buket Kurt
Editor: Şebnem Özdemirci
Design: Tane Mavitan
Illustrated by: Ece Zeber
Translated by: Can Selin Gulel
Editorial consultant: Çiğdem Şimşek

Publisher : Unbound Script
B-10, Seven Wonder Business Center
Plot No. G-20, Basement, Preet Vihar
New Delhi-110092
www.unboundscript.com
books@unboundscript.com

Price : ₹199/-

Printed by
Yash Printographics
Noida, Uttar Pradesh

Despite the short time we were able to spend together,
he planted the seeds of joy of learning in my mind and love,
compassion and courage in my heart.
This book is for my dear father Harun Kurt,
who I still believe is watching me from some places
and giving me the strength...

CHAPER 1
Meeting the "Kid"

Have you ever wanted to see the steps of that first reptile coming out of the sea placing its feet on land for the first time? Or have you ever asked yourself "How do astronauts take care of the "toilet" issues on a zero-gravity space station?" I wonder who came up with the urge to paint the first picture? Whose idea was it to create a particular pattern and start knitting by making yarn using wool? How did the music come on the scene? Architecture and engineering are able to build skyscrapers over a thousand meters and long tunnels under the seas for cars and trains today, have you ever thought which stages they have been through? Why don't the stars fall from the sky? How does the mobile phone work? What were our ancestors afraid of? Why don't the animals on the polar regions feel cold?

If such questions like above appear in your mind, which sometimes can be asked aloud, sometimes not because of your fear of feeling embarrassed or funny, then this book is absolutely for you. Because now I'm going to tell you the story of a very curious child who asks questions just like the ones you read above. Are you ready? Alright then ... Oh sorry, are you asking "Dear author, is it any possible for a child not to ask any questions, or is there a child on Earth who is not even a bit curious about anything?" You are absolutely right! That's what I'm talking about!

- Do you have any crazy questions that you want to know the answers of? So pluck up courage and share your crazy question with everyone, ask it aloud!

- What may "asking a question" lead to? Think of at least three results and picture them in the space below.

So, without further ado, let me start by renewing my introductory sentences to start our story. Now I'm going to tell you a story about a child who you may consider as yourself or one of your friends; me as a child or, one of your parents or teachers, in fact one of any of the adults you ever know. Are you ready? I think it's a more accurate entry now. Let's go!

As I mentioned before, the hero of our story is a child... Name? Does it really matter? You name this child. It can even be your name if you wish. Gender? No! I will not answer this question either, I think this also doesn't matter if it's a boy or a girl[1]. Appearance? I guess I don't want to talk about that either. Don't say "What kind of author is this??" I leave these choices to YOU, I set you free. Let your hero be the child you really want to see through our journey. I call him "The Child", because this child has many more special skills to discover which have valuable impact on the lining of our story.

1 Protogonist of this story "the child" is a genderless character as especially mentioned by the author, There is no masculine or feminen pronouns in Turkish, therefore, for the rest of the story, pronoun assigned for "the child" is "he".

- You want to create an appearance for your hero? Then YOU are the illustrator of this page!

The Child was a third-grade student who was about to be a fourth grader. He had no complaints about the school, not only because he loved to learn and ask questions, but also because he did not have a sibling to play with. Of course, he was not equally interested in all subjects at school. Who can like anything or anyone equally anyway? The Child loved his teacher and his friends very much. I know it's hard to believe but he also loved a couple of subjects and even completing the assignments. Like for example math!

It was his favorite thing to walk around the world of numbers and shapes which are surrounded by unbreakable set of rules. As his knowledge of that world was getting bigger every day, he also felt the knowledge of the universe on his mind was enhancing. The Child also liked science very much. Discovering living and non-living things on the planet and the universe he belonged to, learning the laws of nature, exploring the connections and relations between all the beings was giving him the greatest excitement.

Actually he liked Art and Turkish Language Arts as well. But above all, reading a book... As he wandered through the magical world of books, "I'm glad I learned to read!" he said knowing very well that reading was the greatest power he had. The Child was impressed by one of the sentences his teacher said while she was teaching how to read, "Now that you are learning to read, no one will be able to deceive you kids! Whatever you are curious about, whatever you want to know, you will be able to search and learn about it and have your own ideas." That's exactly how The Child feels about reading.

Speaking of teachers, The Child was lucky indeed. Ms.Deniz loved to ask questions and make the kids ask even many more. Instead of looking at a text and copying it, she always encouraged kids to put down their own independent ideas and thoughts. She would first ask kids to search about the topic before she played the documentary of the unit. Instead of having them solve pages of math problems, she would tell them stories about history of math and ask kids to create their own stories, too. And the chain of events changing The Child's life started with a question asked by his teacher.

Reflection Break

- "All living things in the universe are interconnected." How much do you agree or disagree with the statement above? Put a mark on the table below and think about your reasons.

- Strongly disagree
- Disagree
- Undecided
- Agree
- Strongly agree

- Now... Ask some of your friends also to put a mark on the table below and to share their ideas. After everyone explains their thoughts and ideas, is there a change with your decision? What are the views that changed your mind?

- Strongly disagree
- Disagree
- Undecided
- Agree
- Strongly agree

How would you describe that statement with a picture? Draw a picture below and share it with someone you love.

CHAPER 2
A Class in the Forest

There was less than a month until the last day of school. The Child's probably the favourite unit of science began: "Living things and their relationships." The ecosystem! That morning Ms. Deniz took the class to the forest which was close to school. Each kid had a small notepad, a pencil case, a magnifying glass, tiny zip lock bags and a camera with them. When their teacher told them to prepare those materials for the week's activity, he seized that one of those exciting research tasks was coming soon.

When they arrived forest Ms. Deniz gave the kids only one instruction: "Now kids I just want you to examine your surroundings with careful eyes. You can draw a picture of what you see, take a photo of it, put your ideas or questions in your notebook, and collect some samples and place them in those small bags. Of course, with no harm on any living things that is still alive."

With this highly open-ended instruction, a strong murmur rose from the classroom, fingers raised one by one.

"Can we explain it with a picture, teacher?"
"What are we going to do with the stuff we collect?"
"Do we have to take pictures?"
"Can we just observe?"

The questions were flying in the air. The Child was also excited. Their teacher not only gave them the freedom to work how ever they like but also gave no clue about the task they were going to work on. After staring at those confused faces sheepishly for a while, Ms. Deniz put her hands up in the air like saying "I surrender!". It was like a special password between them. If you put your hands up in the class like this, it would mean "I have something very important to say, I need everyone all ears please!". Hearing their teacher's call, The Child and his friends answered her back by raising their hands one by one. In an instant, silence reigning the forest, nothing could be heard except for the birds, insects and the warm wind.

- What are your favorite subjects you enjoy working on? Why do you think you especially like them more than the others?
- Do you think you are more successful at your most favorite subjects? Can you explain?

Their teacher began speaking calmly not disturbing the sweet natural melody of the silence:

"OK! You are right, alright, everyone is right! I should have been more clear, I know. Well kids, what I want from you is; observe every living creature around you and record every detail by making notes, drawing pictures or taking photos. Later, I will ask you to categorize the information you gathered, but first we will have discussions when we are back in the classroom and then complete our project. If I'm not mistaken one of you asked, "Can we just observe?" Right? My answer will unfortunately be 'No'. Because never forget! Recording the results of the observation is as important as the observing process itself for a scientist. Please consider this as a scientific study. Make sure that you record your observations the way you like."

The Child was very happy. Under the hot sun and warm breeze of may, first he came down on his knees. Encouraged by the effect of the pre-summer warmth on the half-earth-half-grass mixture he felt on his knee, he slowly laid himself down on the ground. All his friends were running in the forest, cheerful, anxious, curious, chirpy. Some already took out their magnifying glasses and started examining a bark, while others were trying to see inside an anthill, struggling on their knees. Some of them were grouped together, helping each other trying to climb a tree, while others had already pulled out their notebooks and crayons, painting the scene right in front of them. Ms. Deniz was walking among the kids, answering questions, reminding them to be careful, watching them with a smile. She was also taking pictures and making notes.

The Child didn't seem to know where to start, but he had to start somewhere anyways. He didn't consider the situation as an assignment or a duty. Also the indecisiveness and sluggishness he was feeling or the rush inside making him restless weren't caused by this project. It was the restlessness triggered by the thought, "There is so much to observe, to see, to know about, to record, to meet, ponder and question." The Child calmly opened his bag, took out his notebook, pencil case and camera. He opened his notebook and as suggested by his teacher, decided to make free- style notes on what he was going to see throughout the day. He paused for a second, "Which one should I start with?". Then he wrote "human" in his notebook in a blink.

- Why do you think the boy recorded the word "human" first?

Why wouldn't the "humans" who were running around excitedly, taking pictures, chasing their teachers asking many questions, those creatures who he had been spending almost the most of his life with, be a part of this research task? Then he picked up his camera, stood up, leaving everything else behind, began to take pictures of his friends, some were climbing a tree, some holding a magnifying glass, examining an insect on the ground with care, while one had been trying to stand up huffing and puffing in dust, right after a stumble and fall caused by a tree root and some of them were making crowns with flowers with joy.

Suddenly he was intrigued by a friend who was very busy trying to stick some leaves in his notebook. Just as he was about to take a step to photograph him closely, he was startled by a hand tapping his shoulder. Turning around, The Child saw his teacher who was staring at him with curious eyes.
Teacher:

"What are you doing kido?"

"I'm working on my research Ms. Deniz."

"I've been watching you all for a while. Everyone dispersed, heading towards flowers, trees, leaves, insects. Even a few of your friends saw a squirrel on a tree. You only photographed us, your friends. Why?"

"You told us to note the creatures we see around us. Isn't a human being a living thing, teacher? I wanted to begin my work by observing human."

Ms. Deniz heehawed while The Child was busy trying to find some meaning behind it, but for some reason she immediately pulled herself together and with a serious tone, asked:

"Well, why did you begin with the human beings kido?"

"I have been feeling very excited since you shared the material list teacher.

"How nice, happy to hear that. Well, what does that have to do with you starting your research with us?"

"First it was unexpected to be surprisingly brought out here in the woods today, plus I got even more excited after we arrived when you assigned us such a task."

The boy was aware that his teacher was looking at him with both interest and blank eyes making him feel that she was already lost.The smile on her face was still there, but she was not as excited as he was. It was like he still wasn't able to express himself enough. For a moment the thought, "Why can't these grown-ups understand us at once?" travelled through his mind. But he had no intention of giving up. He continued his words with determination:

"I mean, teacher, the human beings with great excitement towards learning and discovery caught my attention, I wanted to record this first."

Now she was staring at him as if she was able to follow a bit better. She sweetly touched The Child's shoulder followed by two small pats which aimed to give the feeling of confidence and support:

"Okay," she said. "Continue however you like to."

Reflection Break

Try to imagine the first moments of human beings on the stage of history. Think about the times when there were only plants and animals and people on earth. The times when there were no villages, cities, roads, buildings. Think about the times when there were no social structures, technological or any kind of tools, even the simplest ones.

If our ancestors were not as curious as we are today what kind of a place would the world be? Can you draw a picture and explain why?

What might be the consequences of being curios? Complete the mind map below. Also tell a friend to create their own mind map as well.

BEING CURIOUS

CHAPER 3
A Scientific Study

Arriving back to school, there was a confusion and noise in the classroom. The reason behind the chaos was everyone dying to show each other the photos they took, the observation notes they made and the pictures they drew. The Child was also thrilled with excitement. In addition to taking pictures of his friends, he was also able to capture a moment and took the photo of that little squirrel just before it entered a hollow. A lot of living things with their names and pictures were recorded in the notebook. Grass, sparrow, cat, pine tree, ant, that tall tree which he had no idea about, with its branches hanging almost halfway down its trunk, a cone, a scarab, a daisy, a dandelion, a spider...

With the sound of the maracas silence was all around the class and all eyes were on the teacher.

"I understand your excitement guys, that's exactly what I expect from you at this moment. Sharing your experiences and observations with each other. Because I'm sure you've all seen many different things while you were observing the same location. There were many different sides and points attracted your attention and drew your interest. You now have fifteen minutes. Show us what you've observed, make a small presentation. This presentation of yours must include all the observed and recorded living things which must be categorized considering their common points, none of them will be left out in the cold please."

Fifteen minutes, clock is ticking. "Aww! What's easier than that?" thought The Child. He immediately headed towards the mountain of scrap papers in a box and picked two different colored papers, both used on one side. Since the first day of school, their teacher had been repeating the same sentence, "Because that trees are used to make these papers and forests are our most valuable assets, we should not throw away even a tiny piece of paper in a recycling bin before making the most efficient use of it." So, of course the scrap paper box was quite crowded, and everyone seemed very much used to this meaningful rule.

- How do you think The Child will categorize the living things? Imagine that you are a classmate of these children and you spent a few hours in the woods with them. How would you categorize your records? Show by drawing/writing below. Share your views and explain why?

The Child put the two colored papers side by side and stuck them together. He wrote "LIVING THINGS" right in the middle, in large and colorful letters. He placed two long arrows from below the huge title heading to the sides of the paper, one to the left and the other to the right. In large and colorful letters, he wrote "PLANTS" below one and "ANIMALS" below the other. Then, he carefully drew the creatures he observed and recorded, then put their names in groups. "Grass, pine tree, drooping tree, cone, daisy, dandelion are plants. A human being, sparrow, cat, ant, scarab and spider are animals." He also decorated the poster with small samples of branches and leaves, which he had put in zip lock bags before. He carefully completed his poster and as soon as he was done he looked around with curious eyes.

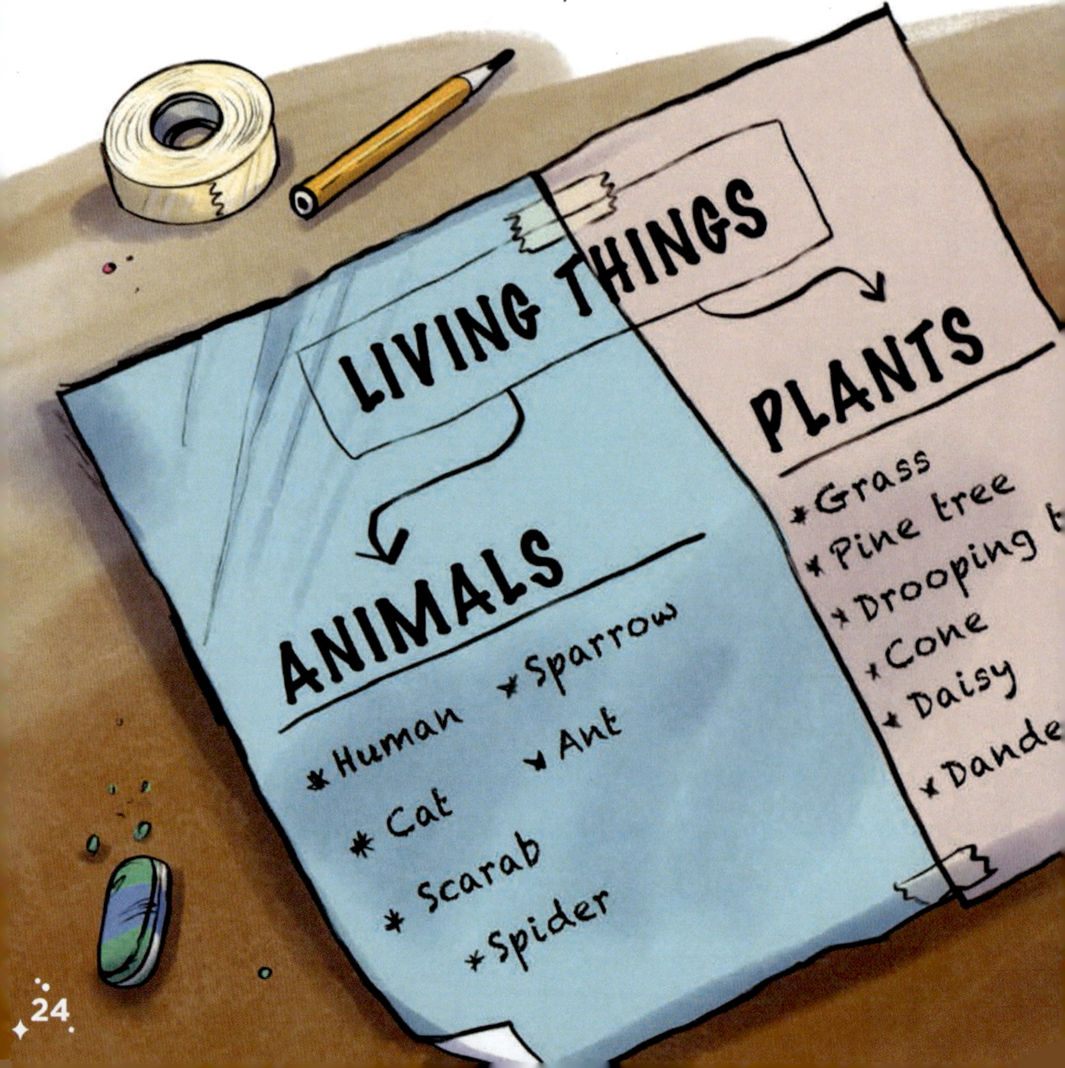

Some of his friends were still working, while others were checking around with curious eyes like himself. Their teacher, on the other hand, was walking among them in silence, when she had a student calling her, she would head there and talk to him/her in a whisper. "Still have time!" thought The Child, and began to prepare for his presentation, quietly reviewing his work.

- Are there similarities and differences between Child's grouping and yours? Can you explain?

CHAPER 4
Thinking Differently

Time was up. Almost everyone was raising their hands excitedly, hoping to share what they had done as soon as possible. There was a formula that their teacher used in such situations. Closing her eyes, randomly pointing at somewhere on the students list, and then it is the time to speak up for the kid whose name just come up. Deniz did so again. She closed her eyes, waved her hand a few times in the air, and placed it on a name. And there exploded the rain of ideas.

"I think my dear friends," said Defne, "living things must be grouped in three. Those who live on land, those who live in the sea and those who live in the air. I know we didn't see any sea creatures today, but this forest might have been by the sea, so I also considered the sea creatures."

"But there is no such thing as living in the air," said Emre in a flash. "This can be called flying and non-flying creatures. All flying creatures also have a home on land."

"Hey kids," their teacher chipped in. "Please let's not interrupt each other. Listen to your friends, when it's your turn, please state the views you agree and disagree with. Thank you Defne and Emre,'' she said and continued picking names.

Aylin was next in line:

"I split living things in two my friends. Those who can move and those who can't. So the grass, those flowers and trees we saw are in group "can't move" and animals are in the group called "can move".

"An interesting perspective Aylin, thank you," said their teacher. ''Plants don't move really? Anyway, we'll be discussing this soon in coming lessons. Let's move on... Yes Duru, you share yours now."

"I split the living things in two, teacher," Duru said. "As plants and animals."

Upon Duru's sharing, a hum rose from the classroom, faces fell. Voices rose "But that's what I've been thinking about, too, that's exactly how I did!"

"Children, calm down! Do not worry, I think this is great," she said.

The Child raised his hand to have a word:

"But teacher, what is great about it! What's the point of our presentations now! Are we going to say the same things?

“I don’t agree with you kids,” said Ms. Deniz. “The thing is, you all have recorded different creatures and let’s see if your records belong to the mentioned groups, we will make a comparison first. The pleasing part is that; science progressed throughout history exactly like this. In disparate corners of the world, different people said the same things and put forward theories, did experiments, and when they arrived at a common agreement, scientific laws began to emerge. Though this would be the next step of our project. Those who share the same idea will work together, so all observations and presentations are very valuable. We will listen to every one of your friends who want to share their ideas, to the end, until they finish, right?”

The Child’s heart was suddenly filled with excitement and joy again. He was wondering how his friends grouped the creatures which he did not notice, but they did. He couldn’t wait to get together now.

"Let’s continue by taking turns to talk," said their teacher. "But first let’s listen to the ones different from the mentioned before, if there is any."

After this sentence, there was only one’s finger reaching out, still hanging in the air. It was Doga.

"Ah-ha, Doga." sighed The Child. Yes, he loved spending time with him, playing games, chatting. However, I think he was also a little bit, a very very tiny bit jealous of him. But not wishing the worst of course. It was as if he was jealous of his mind. Even he himself still couldn’t name this feeling. He had always wanted to know what he would say or do...

"I divided living things into two teacher," said Doga. "Those who can produce their own food and those who have to look for it. Actually, I’m aware I’ll be partners with my friends who categorized living things as plants and animals. Yet that’s the reason why we categorize them that way. Consediring the way of nutrition. I just wanted to explain the point."

Well, The Child suddenly found the reason of his feelings towards his friend. "He thinks differently," he thought. "But how can he do that? I must learn the secret as soon as possible!"

While The Child was lost thinking about Doga's words, he suddenly came to his senses with the voice of his teacher echoing in the class.

"Come on kido! We split into study groups. Join your friends."

Reflection Break

- What does "thinking differently" mean to you? Explain your ideas.
- Are there people in your life who think differently? Who are they? Why do you feel this way about them?
- What do you think the world would be like if all people agreed on everything (thinking alike)? Consider both positive and negative results. List your wedding results on the "T Chart" below. Explain the reasons for the results you listed.

IF EVERYONE THOUGHT THE SAME...

POSITIVE RESULTS	NEGATIVE RESULTS

While you are thinking about an answer, you can start with your close environment. Like your family members, your classmates, your besties...

CHAPER 5
Difficult Questions

All groups completed their work and made a large group presentation by putting their observations together. While they were working, The Child listened to his friends' ideas carefully, felt a little sorry for the creatures he could not see, but thanks to his friends he was happy to learn what he had missed out there. Even he was trying to give all his attention to his friends, he was distracted from time to time and could not help thinking about the question that had stuck in his mind just a period ago. "How does a human being think differently?" He would do anything to know the answer to that question. "Was it in you when you were born or did you gain it later in life? Is there a moment that I think differently from others? Scientists, inventors, explorers... Did they all think differently from others? Or did they just think hard and work hard?" With such questions in his mind and a stare in his eyes, he was rising up out of the classroom and travelling to far far lands. This absent look was noticed by his different-minded friend, Doga. With the impact of Doga's touch on his back, The Child felt as if he suddenly ended his journey and fell back into the classroom.

"Hey! You've been so quiet for a while; you've been wandering off. What have you been thinking?"

"I've been thinking about thinking."

"Hmm," said Doga in a serious manner. "From what point have you been thinking about thinking? "

For some reason, The Child thought that Doga would throw a laugh at him or give him one of those famous smart answers of his. He liked being taken seriously by his favorite smart friend. "Of course, you have to learn from the expert!" he thought.

"For example you," said The Child. "How do you do that?"

"What? You mean thinking? Everyone thinks, it's unstoppable. In fact, not only we humans but also animals have the ability to think."

"I know that, Doga. Your way of thinking is much different. How do you do that?" "

"Different from what?"

"From everyone I know, all the kids in the class. From me!"

The Child softly bowed his head looking away from his friend. He thought his curiosity would be misunderstood, like as if he was jealous or something. Oh no. He blushed.

"How nice to hear that from you! Thank you."

This time Doga's face was starting to turn slightly pink. Obviously these kids weren't very good at receiving compliments. But Doga quickly came back down to earth. He really wanted to continue this very much interesting conversation:

"What do you mean by thinking differently?"

"To be able to see what nobody can see, to be able to interpret things differently from everyone else. Well, things like that..."

"I love reading books and watching documentaries."

"Me, too," said The Child excitedly. 'But almost all kids love these stuff, what's the deal?"

"Actually as you learn new things, new questions pour into mind, then more new questions and more. So I guess, you think more and you think in a variety. You also, my friend, should be fair to yourself.

"What do you mean?" asked The Child. Doga continued his words:

"For example, I heard what you were talking about with our teacher today. You know, your tiny conversation about why you primarily started your project with observing us. I think that was a quite different point of view."

"Wow! How nice to hear that from you! And I thank you, too," said The Child.

They started laughing.

"You also ask difficult questions. Thought-provoking questions! Thanks to you, from this day on I'll be thinking a lot about this different thinking," said Doga.

"Tell me If you find the answer, okay?"

- What is the criteria that makes a question "difficult"?
- Think about the issues/areas in your life that have challenged you the most. Then think about the situations that you used to have difficulties but now are easier for you to deal with. What do you think is "the concept"sues?

CHAPER 6
Eternal Curiosity

All groups presented their works. Everyone listened to each other with curiosity, asked questions and made comments. After these few lessons with their teacher, asking many questions and searching for answers, the day continued with lunch, followed by the art and IT lessons. Of course, we should not forget the enjoyable recesses of the last days of spring. They would be together with Ms Deniz again for the last two classes at the end of the day. Before their teacher left for a few hours, "We're not done with our research yet, guys! I have a surprise for you in the last two lessons. Everybody be prepared with your notebooks and pencil cases with you and wait for me, okay? We will have another lesson outside the classroom again!" she said.

"Where are we going, teacher?" "To the forest again?" "What are we going to do?"

"You guys are amazing, always keep curious like this." she said and she left the classroom smiling, without answering any questions.

The Child's eyes were filled with love and admiration while he was watching his teacher walking away. "Ms. Deniz, she rocks..." he thought. She was good at exciting her students indeed. Humanity wouldn't be able to go even a step forward without the enthusiasm for learning new things.

Reflection Break

The famous philosopher, educator, and writer Confucius, who is estimated to have lived in China between 551 BC and 479 BC, said, "Learning without thinking is wasted effort."

What do you think Confucius might be trying to convey with this phrase? Share your thoughts and listen to your friend's/family's opinions on this topic.

getting thirsty	filling your bottle	drinking water
learning/ knowing	wondering	thinking

Yukarıda yer alan kavramları incele.

1) Think about the connection between the phrases on the first line.

2) Now try to see a connection between the concepts on the second line.

3) Match the phrases on line one and concepts on line two (one phrase may match only one concept)

4) With which of the diagrams on the next page would you explain the relationship between the concepts of learning/knowing, wondering, and thinking? Why?

WONDERING
THINKING
LEARNING/ KNOWING

WONDERING
THINKING
LEARNING/ KNOWING

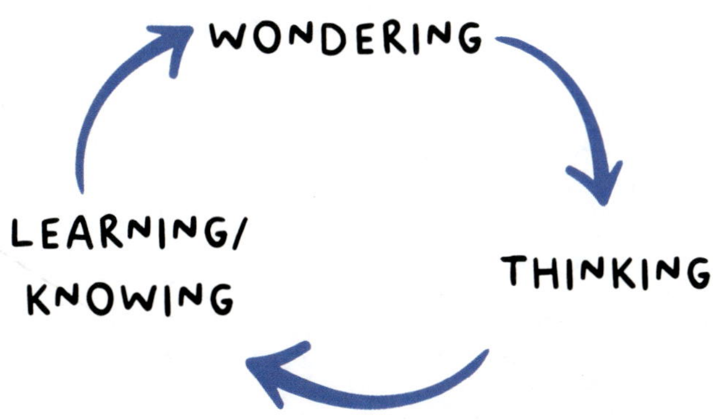
WONDERING
THINKING
LEARNING/ KNOWING

CHAPER 7
Hello Philosophy

The moment has come. As soon as they heard the recess bell, the most enthusiastic class joining back to the classroom, probably the only one, was 3-D. They were back in the classroom, getting in line with their notebooks and pencil cases in their hands, as their teacher told them to do. Just after the teacher's bell, Ms. Deniz appeared at the door. Seeing her students prepared to go, waiting in line, she let out a small laugh. Then she added:

"You are wonderful, my children! I'm proud of you. If you're ready, let's head to the library. It seems you little scientists are ready for the last research task of the day!"

So The Child and his friends made their way to the library with curious steps and sat around tables in silence. The Child watched his friends for a while, looking around with bright eyes. Next year would be his last year with his classmates. Of course, with Ms Deniz, too. These thoughts were sometimes making him feel sad. He remembered their first year in school. He remembered how they scanned each other and their teacher with timid eyes. They were also having arguments when they were trying to get to know each other. Sometimes they broke each other's hearts. But hey, such things could happen between people trying to be friends. Those were the days they argued about where to sit when they arrive the library. It could take even ten minutes for them to settle in. Not to mention the noise they were making, already forgotten where they were. But in time they made a great team. A team of members who listened to each other well, emphatasie, put effort to cover little mistakes and help each other when needed. Most importantly, they loved each other. "Love conquers all," said Ms Deniz. "People who love each other are also tolerant and respectful to each other. And remember kids, everyone is worth loving. "You can see a likeable side in each person, even there is only one, as long as you look for that particular likeable side with care." She was right!

- "You can see a likeable side in each person, even there is only one, as long as you look for that particular likeable side with care." Do you agree with Ms Deniz' statement about love?

- We are criticized by many people in our lives. This sometimes make us forget our own positive traits. Come on, love yourself a little today. Look in the mirror, smile at yourself and picture this smiling face. Put everything you like about yourself around your self-portrait.

- If there are people you think usually forget about their positive sides, this time, you can draw portraits considering their lovely sides. Let's see what their reaction will be when you share their positive qualities.

While The Child was thinking about these things, his eyes connected with his teacher's. Ms Deniz winked at him, as if she was asking "What's on your mind?". The Child, on the other hand, shrugged his shoulders as if he was answering back "Nothing..." and bowed his head with a smile. Ms Deniz started to speak:

"Guys, I know you worked hard today and you are very tired. Now, if you feel ready, you will have one last little research task. If you are tired, we can have a free reading time and relax altogether to the end of the day."

"No, teacher!"

"Let's do research!"

"You made us very curious!"

"Please teacher, come on, tell us, come oon!"

"Okay, okay," said Ms Deniz. "Your task is to find out the person who classified living things with a scientific perspective for the first time in history. Plus, what kind of classification did s/he make? Now here's your clue, this person is a very, very important one. I'm also curious if you have some common points with that person? You would like to learn that too, wouldn't you?"

All the children were whispering excitedly among themselves. Ms Deniz had her answer. The murmur in the air absolutely meant "Yes, we would like that!"

"Then come on chop chop. You do your research whether on computers or with the books. I'm waiting here, find the answer and come near me."

The children suddenly stood up like a flock of birds taking off from the ground and flew all over the library. Their school had a rich library. Moreover, they knew how to use it. Gokce taught them where to find what among hundreds of encyclopedias, fairy tales, novels, poems or source books. Gokce was actually the library teacher, but she was like a big sister for the whole school. Behind her desk right at the entrance of the library, always smiling through her round glasses with her hazel eyes, she welcomed every one of the children. She kept track of the borrowed books, recorded the new ones, and sometimes came to their rescue when they needed to do a research like this. That's why she was already surrounded by a group of children. Gokce, on the other hand, was typing keywords in the search engine, trying to answer all questions, recommending books and encyclopedias where they could find answers.

The Child also loved reading encyclopedias and investigating their pages. Encyclopedias written especially for children were wonderful. Thanks to Ms Deniz, she created such curiosity that The Child had no more patience to wait for the long queue in front of Gokce or go through an encyclopedia. His steps leaded him directly to the computers. "I'll find the answer first, then I'll read the encyclopedia thoroughly," he thought.

They could only have the access to some online encyclopedias on those computers. The Child clicked on one of them excitedly and typed the words in the search tab: "First person to classify animals." The moment he hit the magnifying glass, names and links started to load on the page. These links would lead him to new pages. The Child began to read carefully, one by one. The sentence "History of the classification (taxonomy) of animals" in the third link would have led him to the answer he was looking for. He clicked on it.

Yessss! The answer he was looking for was in the first paragraph he was reading: Aristotle! The name sounded familiar. Their teacher should have mentioned it before for sure. Or it was in one of the books he read. He immediately clicked on the name so he could recognize who it was. He eagerly waited for the page to load. Before he started reading, he carefully examined a stone bust that he was suddenly face to face. Was that him? Since he doesn't have a photograph, he must have lived in very, very ancient times. The first sentence he read left him with a new question: "One of the greatest philosophers in the history of philosophy and also an important scientist."

Of course he knew the word scientist. A person who deals with any branch of science and studies the subject through researches. How many times, even today, Ms Deniz called them, "Little scientists!". What about the term philosopher? In fact, The Child had heard this word many times before, both from his family and teacher, but until now, perhaps he wasn't curious enough about its meaning.

The Child stood up in a rush and ran up to his teacher with huge excitement. without turning off the computer or writing anything in the notebook.

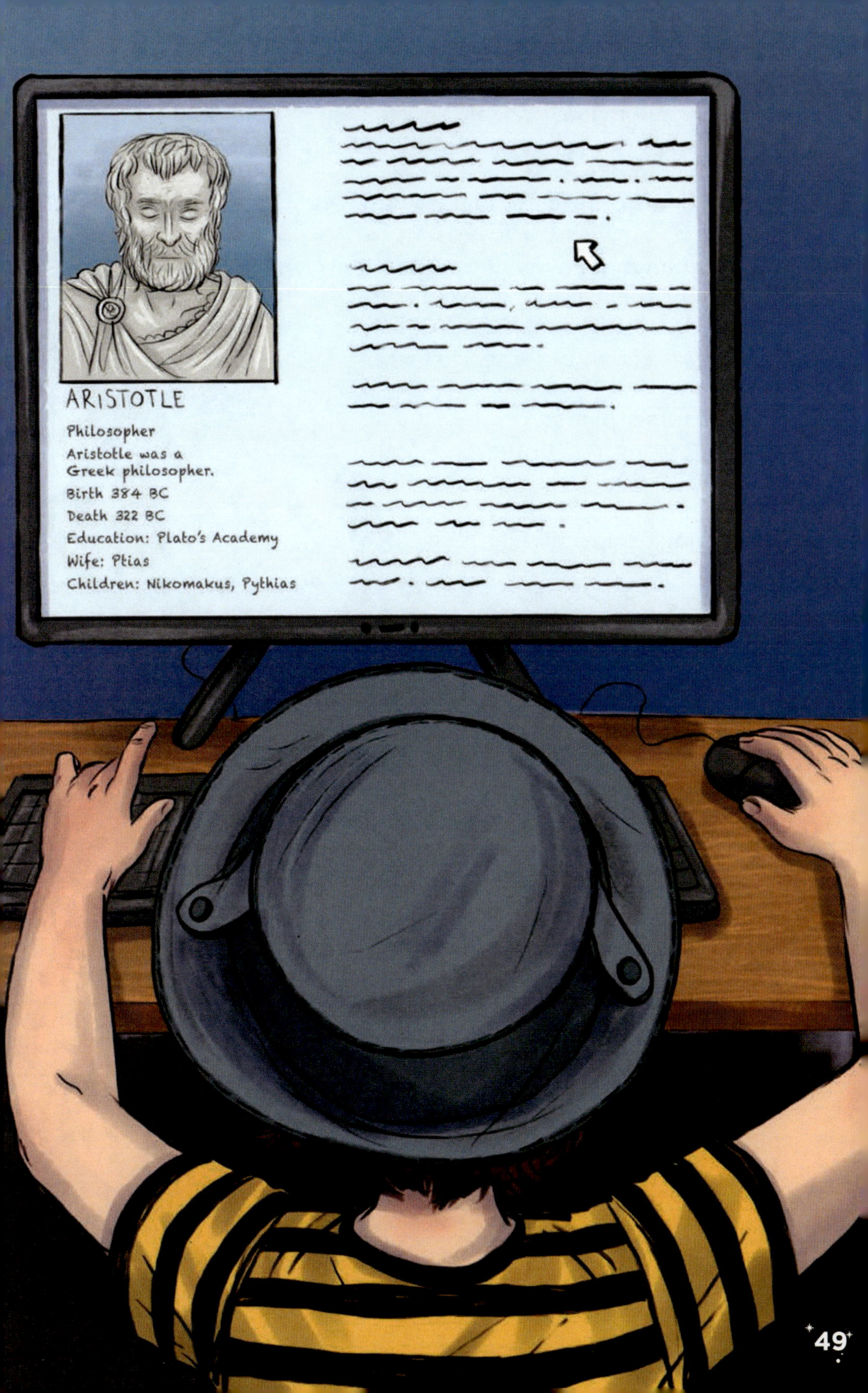
ARISTOTLE
Philosopher
Aristotle was a Greek philosopher.
Birth 384 BC
Death 322 BC
Education: Plato's Academy
Wife: Ptias
Children: Nikomakus, Pythias

"I've found it, teacher, I've found it!"

"Yeey! Tell me. Who is it?"

"Aristo, Aristotal, something like that. Oh no, I forgot to take notes because of excitement."

"You're amazing kido, what a speed," said Deniz Teacher. "Your answer is correct, Aristotle. But for now, don't tell anyone, okay? Look how enthusiastically your friends are working on their research and you Mr., you start making some notes.

"Okay teacher, but can I ask you something first?"

"Of course, please."

"What is a philosopher, teacher?"

After thinking for a while;

"People who seek for wisdom in the universe are called the philosophers. " she said.

This answer gave birth to a new question in the child's mind:

"But what is philosophy?"

His teacher replied without hesitation:

"Like what you are doing right now, asking questions, looking for answers and thinking. "

"Does that mean I'm a philosopher now?" asked The Child and excitedly, without breathing, he listed new questions one after another:

"Is there anyone in this life who does not even think, wonder or seek answers? So all the human beings are philosophers then? But why did the... "

"Stop, chill out kido." Ms Deniz interrupted. "Are you sure there isn't anyone in your family who can answer your questions accurately?"

"Of course!" said The Child.

He recalled a moment with his mom, he asking: "Mom, what does my grandfather do? Whenever we go in his house, I find him reading or writing something " and she answering "Your grandfather is a retired philosophy professor."

"You're right, teacher, thank you very, very much," he said and headed towards the computer room. But no minutes would pass with this impatience inside him until he arrived home and gave an immediate call to his grandpa.

Reflection Break

- Shall we go back to a moment in the story?

While the child was thinking about these things, his eyes connected with his teacher's. Ms Deniz winked at him, as if she was asking "What's on your mind?". The child, on the other hand, shrugged his shoulders as if he was answering back "Nothing..." and bowed his head with a smile.

- We've been thinking all day; we are so tired. As we are getting closer to the end of our story, shall we take a subtle shrug and a "Nothing!" break? Then please follow the steps below,

Now take a comfy position. You may sit in a chair, place your head on a table or lie down on your bed.

We're not going to do anything for a minute, are you ready? You can set a one-minute alarm if you wish, you may set your alarm for of course many more minutes if you like to do more "nothing".

Now start the time and close your eyes. Enjoy the moments you are going to spend doing "Nothing." Just breathe in and out and not do anything else.

I think your alarm went off, so let's think about the time you spent...

- How did you spend that one minute? Did you really succeed to do nothing?

- If your answer is no, can you explain what you experienced during this time period? I'm sure your mind kept working even you tried so hard to keep your body still. Can you draw a picture of this one minute of your mind below?

- Do you think "thinking" is a stoppable action? Are there moments in which we do not think of even a thing? Can you explain?

CHAPER 8
A Sudden Enter

Dilek had a quick look at the kitchen clock. It was five past four. "He should have been here ten minutes ago," she thought, but it was an early stage for a panic. "He's definitely stuck in traffic jam, he's on the way, almost home," she sighed, turning off the oven. The kitchen smelled like cheese pastries. "I'm taking the buns out so they cool a bit," she muttered. She opened the oven, put on her glove, and just as she was about to lean forward and hold the tray, the doorbell began to ring stubbornly. Dazzled by the insistent doorbell, Dilek would almost hurt her hand. She hurried to the door. Dozens of bad thoughts flooded her mind in a few seconds. As soon as she opened the door, The Child burst in and threw his bag on the floor "Plup!" and took off his shoes, tossing one to the left other to the right, far and away from each other. Meanwhile, Dilek was staring at The Child sheepishly with a dull expression on her white face.

The Child rushed into the house without even saying a "Hello!". He went to his room and grabbed his small laptop and came back in a flash.

"Dilek, let's video call my grandfather. Please! Come on!"

"Something bad happened?" Dilek asked. Her voice echoed highly and fully alarmed.

Thanks to her reaction, since he entered the house, The Child literally looked at her face for the first time.

"Nea, I was just going to ask him something important. Are you okay, Dilek? You look like you saw a ghost."

"You freaked the hell out of me kido!," said Dilek.

Dilek pulled herself together as if she suddenly woke up from a dream. The blank look on her face was now replaced by two frowning brows. She began to quickly list her reproachful sentences:

"Do you ring a bell like that really? Do you enter your house saying nothing! My eye was already on the clock; you were on my mind just because you were a little late. I was very scared when the bell shrieked wildly. And when you rushed in and asked about Uncle Selim... Sweetheart, can you imagine what I've been through in my mind? Don't you never, ever ..."

"Okay, I'm sorry Dilek, you have a right, it's not fair. I'm just a tiny bit excited, that's all, believe me, I didn't mean to scare you," he said and they hugged each other tightly.

At that moment The Child could feel Dilek's heart pounding against his chest. He felt very sorry for frightening her this much and hugged her even more tighter. "She loves me very much. " he thought.

Dilek was actually a university student living with her roommate upstairs. The Child and Dilek both started "first grade" at the same time. Of course she was a young woman studying at the conservatory, and he was a little sweet first grader, it was just a funny little joke between them. The Child's parents used to arrive home from work almost around half past six or seven. Until that time, Dilek was taking care of the child, they would have a snack together, chat, do homework, and play games in the rest of the time. Dilek thus felt lucky and proud that she was able to save some pocket money and continue her school without being a burden for her family, plus she had a job she loved so much.

"Well... It's your turn," Dilek broke the silence. She stood up slowly, her hands on her waist and frowned as she continued. "What is this important question you want to ask Uncle Selim? Pardon my curiosity but is it something important which may cause a severe shock?"

She was striking her fake "I am so angry right now!" pose. Despite the pose, there was always an obviously hidden smile on her face.

"Okay, I'll tell you, but first let me ask you something."

"What is it?" "

"What does a wildly shrieking bell mean? As far as I can remember, our bell sings absolutely like a bird."

"Quickly to the bathroom you little tornado!" Dilek started chasing her. The Child had already swooshed to the bathroom and closed the door. He could still hear Dilek's voice, which was giving sweet orders

"First, wash up, then go change. Have a couple of these delicious pastries and finish your orange juice. Only then you can call your grandfather!"

CHAPER 9
Meeting Grandpa the Philosopher"

Grandpa Selim was a recently retired philosophy professor who had left the university two years ago. Before he retired, approximately five-six years ago, he and his lovely wife, Granny Leyla, bought a house in a small town Kucukkuyu in the Ayvacik district of Canakkale. They had been able to spend only a few weeks in summers since then. The Child's grandmother was a teacher retired a long time ago, but his grandfather kept on working in summer, travelling to a variety of cities to join philosophy events and continued to teach youngsters. However, at the end of last summer, they had made a sudden decision and announced that they decided to start a life there. The Child of course was frustrated by the decision. He was used to seeing them several times a week, but now... he wouldn't be able to come together with his grandparents more than a few times in a whole year! Can you imagine?

He was convinced after listening to the long list of reasons about the city sucking life out of them, as a solution, they often connected online, smiling to the camera.

The Child's eyes lit up when he saw his grandfather's face appearing on the screen.

"Heey grandpa, how are you? I missed you so much."

"Oh my sweetheart, my one and only. How nice to hear these from you."

"Where is granny?"

"She went down to neighbor for a 5 o'clock coffee. It's just me, alright?"

"Sure pups! I want to talk to you about something important."

"What is it for god's sake? Now you got my interest."

The Child told his grandfather about his day elaborately, starting from early minutes of the morning, without skipping a detail. Their research in the forest, the conversation he had with his teacher on human beings, what he shared with his friend Doga, their presentations, what his teacher said about his friends with similar perspectives, and finally their dialogue in the library. Grandpa Selim listened to his grandson carefully without interruption. Then the Child:

"Look grandpa, actually you already got the questions I want to ask you, but I'll start with my first question anyway. Are you a philosopher?"

Grandpa Selim laughed out loud.

"No dear, it's not that easy to be a philosopher. I can call myself a philosophist, at best."

"Why? Are you any different from Aristotle?

"Ah! I appreciate it my child, but our differences are infinite. And these are not questions to be answered from this much distance."

"But grandpa," said The Child in frustration. He was a little bit disappointed. "How excited I was to learn all the answers from you."

"Come on kido! Wouldn't life be so boring if we learned all the answers at once? A philosopher is a person who spends his entire life searching for wisdom. See, I've already answered one of your questions, too."

"And what do you think about this 'thinking different' thing? At least say that."

"Okay, we're going to start our philosophy classes with you this summer, you're ready now. It's obvious, no more words needed."

"Whooaa! Grandpa! Summer is so far and away!"

"Come on, it's not a big deal kido, schools will be closed in three weeks. We were actually going to surprise you, but now I feel like I have to spill the beans now. Otherwise, you seem to explode like a volcano right in front of me.''

Grandpa Selim was laughing mysteriously.

"Come on grandpa, tell me. What is it?"

"You can hang out with us here all summer, if you like?"

Dilek came down running after the huge scream she heard while she was reading her book next door.

"Dilek! I will spend this whole summer with my grandparents. Three months, exactly three months! Yeaaeeeyyy!!!''

The Child was dancing with joy, jumping here and there, howling with genuine happiness. With the joyful celebration screams in the background:

"Hello, Dilek," said the sweet voice.

"Hello, Uncle Selim," Dilek replied. "I have some complaints about your grandson, there has been some excitement, some panic around since he arrived home today. He made my heart dropped, for your information."

Grandpa Selim laughed and replied:

"This is the excitement of being curious and learning new things, Dilek. It drags people into an enthusiastic madness. I am proud of you my curious kido!"

- Think about the last sentence of grandpa Selim? How does learning new things make you feel? Please explain.

At the end of this long, exciting, tiring day full of surprises in every minute, it was time for The Child to go to bed. His parents neatly tucked him in, kissed him and said good night. They smiled at the door before turning off the light. "Sweet Dreams!" said his mother. They turned off the lights, closed the door and left. With the light turned off, dozens of luminous stars and planets on the ceiling began to glow. Every night, The Child would look at the ceiling before he went to sleep, sometimes thinking what a day it was, sometimes dreaming about the future, and sometimes wishing well for himself and everyone he loved, and he would fall asleep.

That night, there was one specific dream about the future; the wonderful summer he was going to spend with his grandparents and the philosophy classes which were approved by grandpa in terms of the right timing.

If he knew that the lessons would start under a starry sky like the ceiling he is looking at now, he probably would have spent three weeks with insomnia caused by excitement. But how would he be able to know? Well, you know we can learn particular things only when we truly experience them.

Last Reflection Break

- How do you think the story will continue?
- Why do you think the philosophy lessons will start under the "shining" sky?
- What do you think about the statement? "We can learn particular things only when we truly experience them."
- If you don't agree with the statement, support your ideas with at least three examples of incidents.
- If you agree with the statement, support your ideas with at least three examples of incidents.

Don't forget to share your thoughts on these questions as you have done so far like the others in this book and listen to the opinions of different people with care. See you in the next story. Goodbye for now, stay curious, stay "Child" ...

THE END

BUKET KURT

She was born in Balıkesir on a December morning, yet lived in Kocaeli until she started university in İzmir. During and after the education years, she has always been interested in acting and singing as an amateur, also very much into reading and writing. Learning has always been her passion as she has always been in love with math, science and nature.

When it was time to choose one of these fields as a profession, becoming a teacher was the best way to enjoy them all at once. After her unfortunate departure from the master's study at Philosophy department, she could not stay away from the world of "Child Philosophy" and continued her studies individually. She worked at schools in Istanbul, authorized by IBO, for eleven years, as primary years' homeroom teacher, curriculum development specialist, child philosophy instructor and academic leader. She also directed studies on children's rights and discrimination. One day she decided to follow her dreams, said goodbye to the big city chaos and moved to a village in İzmir. She started a new life as a teacher in the middle of forests, rivers and mountains.

She lives in Selçuk with her buddy Fındık and keeps on learning and having fun together with children, continues making up stories and telling them with great enthusiasm every single day.

ECE ZEBER

A literate illustrator. She learned drawing from her parents. She graduated from the art de-partment of a high school in Balıkesir. She studied animation at Eskişehir Anadolu University. While she was working as an animation designer in different studios as a character and backg-round developer, she realized that working regularly in an office was not fulfilling enough for her. After her unfortunate departure from the master's study at the Animation department, she dedicated herself to children's books. She is a holistic mystic spirit and loves antiques, but this has nothing to do with the topic. She's currently working at her personal home office with her husband, getting prepared for the new projects coming.

Can Selin GULEL

Ms Selin made the decision of her life when she was 10 and became an English teacher. However, at high school, she experienced talk radio, learned post-production, then started hosting the worldwide popular kids show, Disney Club, from Paris and Orlando, for television, worked for a variety of media including TV series, commercials, documentaries and talk shows, edited news, wrote articles for magazines, created puppet theatres while she was attending her classes at the university. After graduation she started working as a teacher both in a kindergarten in the mornings and at the university in the afternoons. After a couple of years, she continued learning and teaching in a variety of primary, secondary and high schools. Her priority in language teaching is to make learners feel enthusiastic and happy, to open up some room for comfort and joy, therefore confidence and success.
She lives with her cat/tiger Tarço in İstanbul. She is in love with the universe and all the beings. She is one of the curious, hilarious and vivacious ones.